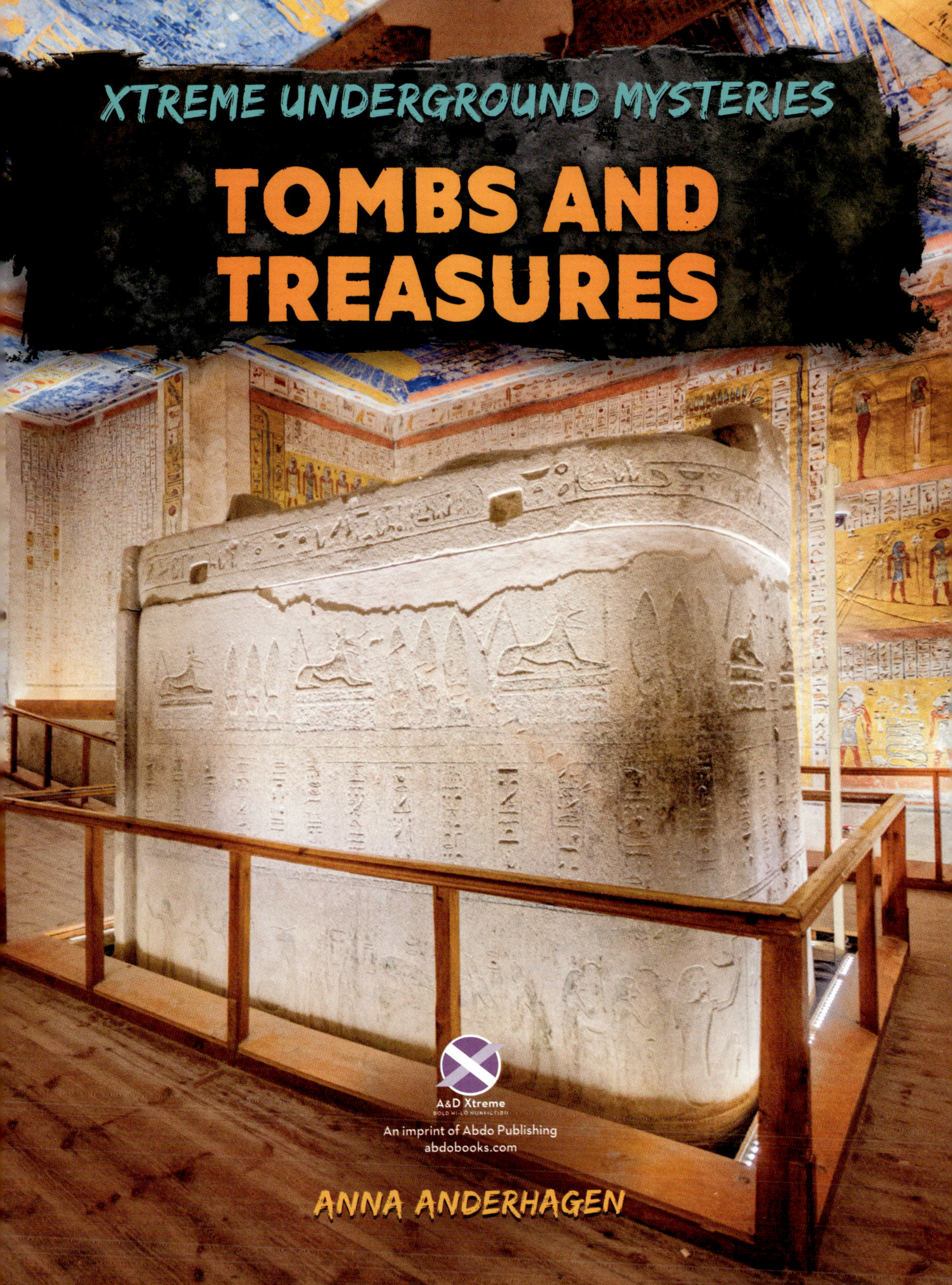

XTREME UNDERGROUND MYSTERIES

TOMBS AND TREASURES

A&D Xtreme
An imprint of Abdo Publishing
abdobooks.com

ANNA ANDERHAGEN

TAKE IT TO THE XTREME!

GET READY FOR AN EXTREME ADVENTURE! THE PAGES OF THIS BOOK WILL TAKE YOU INTO THE WONDROUS WORLD BENEATH YOUR FEET. WHEN YOU HAVE FINISHED READING THIS BOOK, TAKE THE XTREME CHALLENGE ON PAGE 45 ABOUT WHAT YOU'VE LEARNED!

ABDOBOOKS.COM
Published by Abdo Publishing, a division of ABDO, PO Box 398166, Minneapolis, Minnesota 55439.

Printed in the United States of America, North Mankato, MN.
102025
012026

THIS BOOK CONTAINS RECYCLED MATERIALS

Design: Kelly Doudna, Mighty Media, Inc.
Production: Mighty Media, Inc.
Editor: Katherine Chu

Cover Photograph: Matyas Rehak/Adobe Stock
Interior Photographs: BabelStone/Wikimedia Commons, pp. 36–37; Carol M. Highsmith/Library of Congress, pp. 40–41; DiscoA340/Wikimedia Commons, pp. 42–43; Donnebryant/Shutterstock, p. 26; Efired, pp. 16–17; Fedor Selivanov/Shutterstock, pp. 22–23; GEKKON [Maksym Tsalko]/Adobe Stock, pp. 24–25; Goyo Conde/Adobe Stock, pp. 8–9; InnerPeace/Adobe Stock, pp. 14–15; Internet Archive Book Images/Wikimedia Commons, pp. 32–33; Irina Kononova/Shutterstock, pp. 10–11; ItsStuffy/Shutterstock, pp. 38–39; Jaroslav Moravcik/Adobe Stock, pp. 4–5, 12–13; konstantant/Adobe Stock, pp. 20–21; Laura Passavanti/Adobe Stock, p. 44; Matyas Rehak/Adobe Stock, p. 1; Nic McPhee/Wikimedia Commons, p. 35 (bottom); Object 194654. Courtesy of the Penn Museum. www.penn.museum, p. 34; Rjcastillo/Wikimedia Commons, p. 27; SL-Photography/Shutterstock, pp. 28–29; The New York Times photo archive/Wikimedia Commons, p. 9; © The Trustees of the British Museum, p. 35 (top); Vitsuha/Wikimedia Commons, pp. 18–19; Wikimedia Commons, pp. 6–7; Yasemin Olgunoz Berber/Shutterstock, pp. 30–31
Design Elements: tsayuet/Adobe Stock (rocky texture); Tunatura/Adobe Stock (tunnel texture)

LIBRARY OF CONGRESS CONTROL NUMBER: 2025939065
PUBLISHER'S CATALOGING-IN-PUBLICATION DATA
Names: Anderhagen, Anna, author.
Title: Tombs and treasures / by Anna Anderhagen
Description: Minneapolis, Minnesota : Abdo Publishing, 2026 | Series: Xtreme underground mysteries | Includes online resources and index.
Identifiers: ISBN 9781098297817 (lib. bdg.) | ISBN 9798384930624 (ebook)
Subjects: LCSH: Tombs--Juvenile literature. | Archaeology--Juvenile literature. | Geosciences--Juvenile literature. | Earth sciences--Juvenile literature.
Classification: DDC 393.1--dc23

CONTENTS

CHAPTER 1

GLINTS OF GOLD

Archaeologist Howard Carter just uncovered a new Egyptian tomb. He held a candle to peer inside. Gold flashed in the candlelight. Treasures beyond imagination had sat untouched for thousands of years. Carter had just found Pharaoh Tutankhamun's (King Tut's) tomb!

The first room in King Tut's tomb was called the antechamber. It took Carter and his workers more than two months to remove and record 600 artifacts from the antechamber.

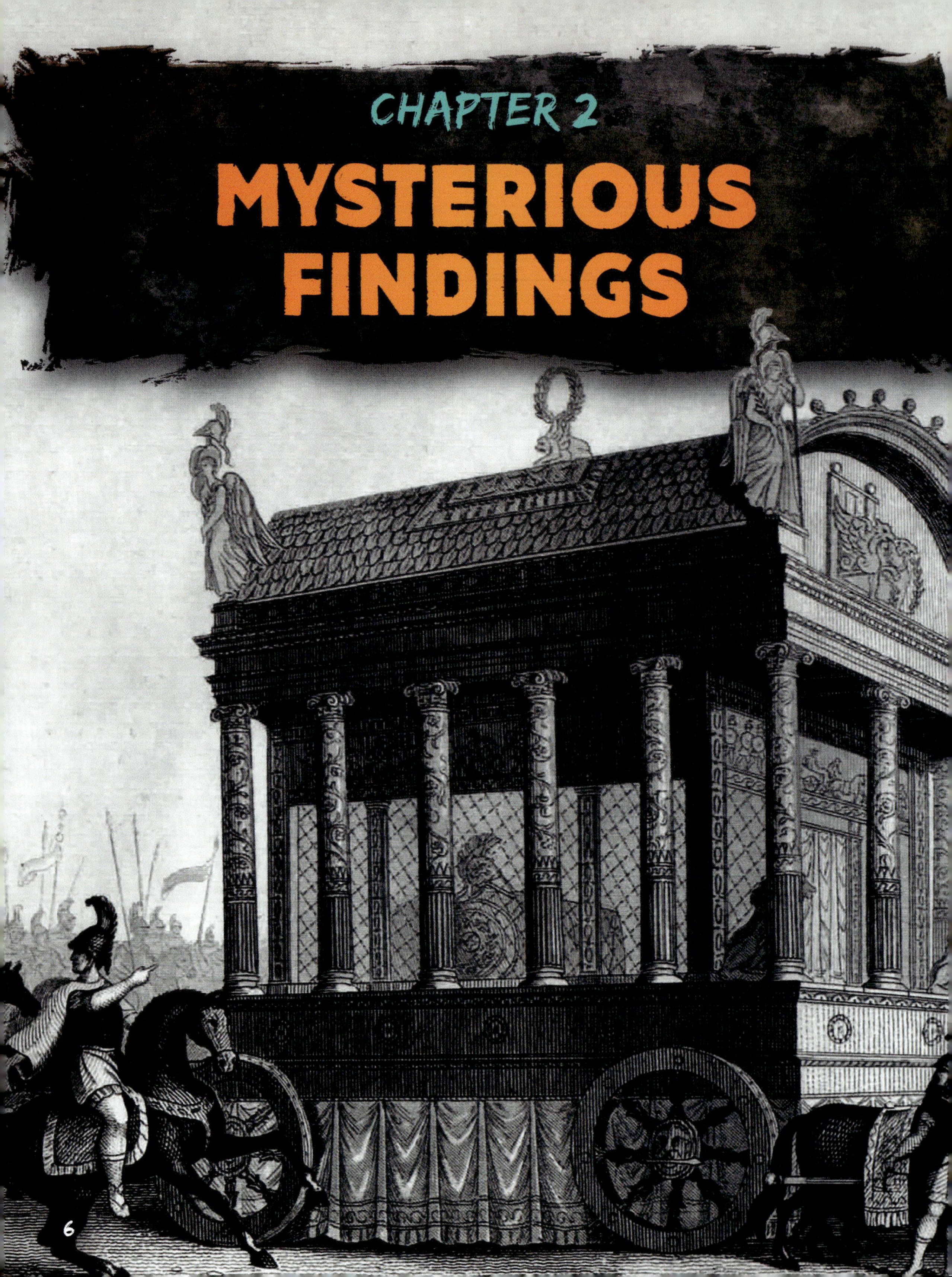

CHAPTER 2

MYSTERIOUS FINDINGS

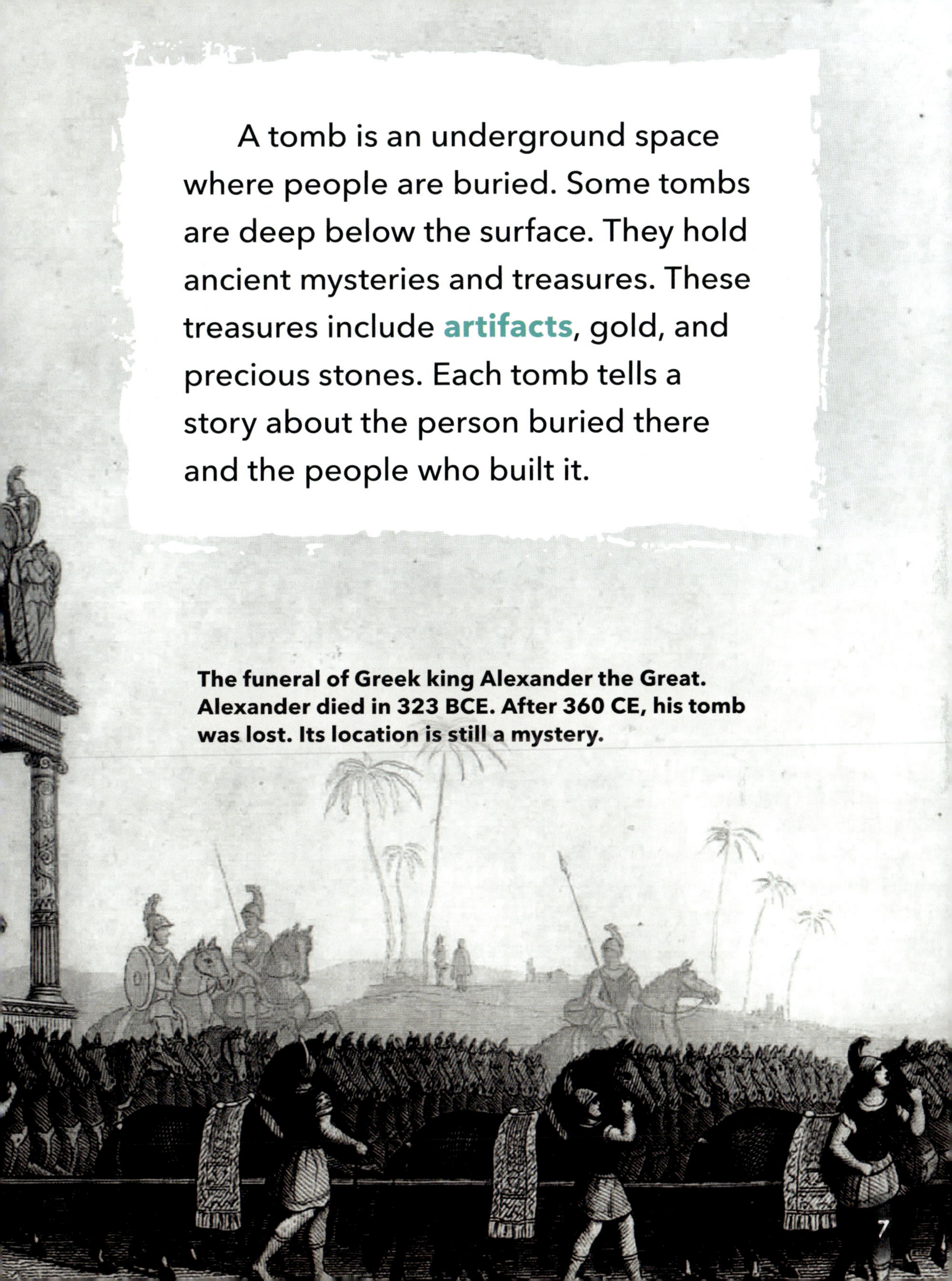

A tomb is an underground space where people are buried. Some tombs are deep below the surface. They hold ancient mysteries and treasures. These treasures include **artifacts**, gold, and precious stones. Each tomb tells a story about the person buried there and the people who built it.

The funeral of Greek king Alexander the Great. Alexander died in 323 BCE. After 360 CE, his tomb was lost. Its location is still a mystery.

CHAPTER 3

TUTANKHAMUN'S TOMB

George Herbert, Earl of Carnarvon, hired Carter in 1907. Carter's job was to find tombs in Egypt's Valley of the Kings. In 1922, he found King Tut's tomb.

King Tut's tomb had four rooms. The rooms held gold-covered **chariots**, furniture, **jewelry**, a solid gold mask, and more.

XTREME FACT

Herbert died from a mosquito bite six months after King Tut's tomb was found. Some people believe a curse from opening the tomb caused his death.

Carter (*left*) spent almost 10 years removing more than 5,000 objects from King Tut's tomb.

There are at least 62 tombs in Egypt's Valley of the Kings.

A copy of King Tut's coffin. King Tut had three coffins, or boxes that held his body. His inner coffin was solid gold. It weighed 243 pounds (110 kg)!

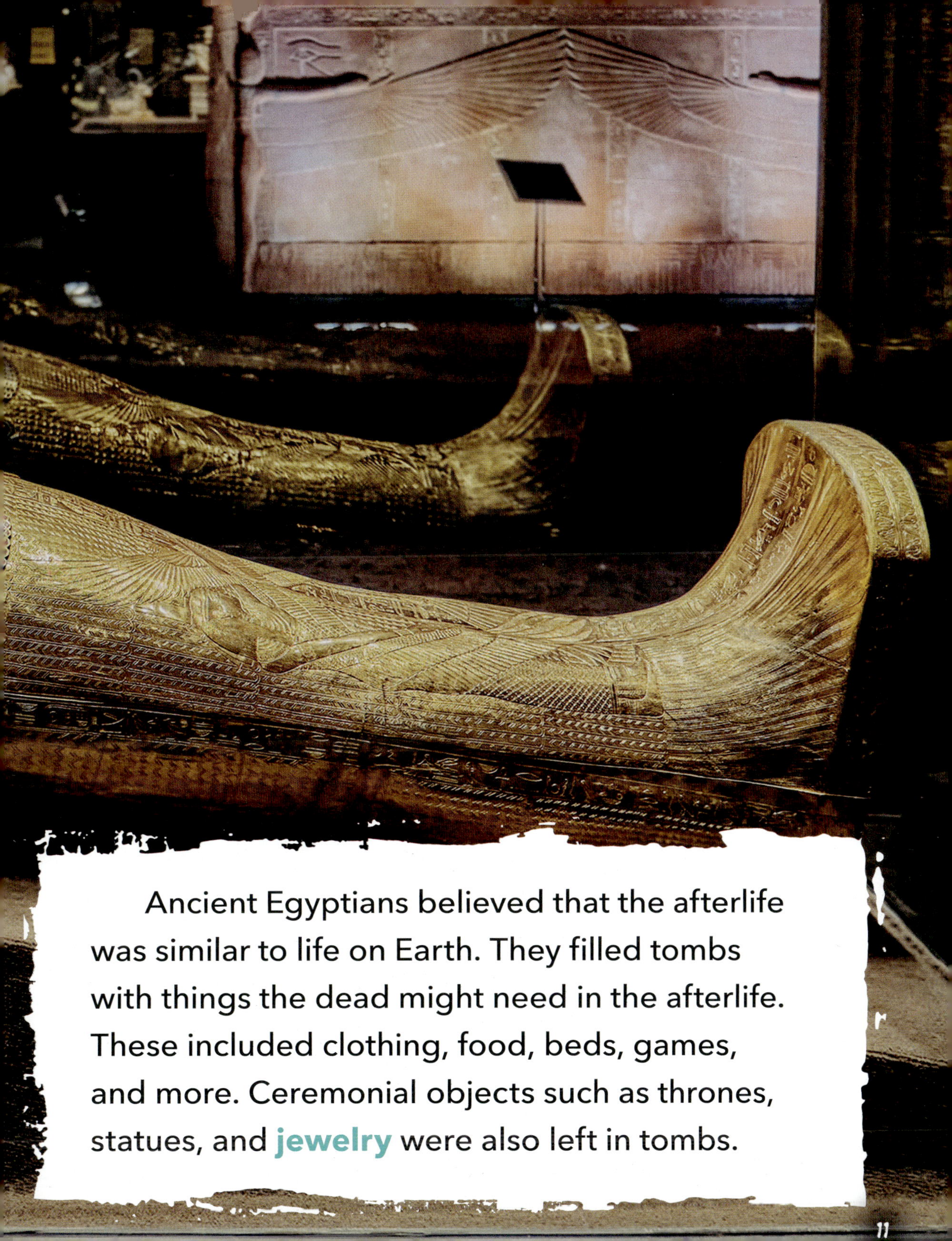

Ancient Egyptians believed that the afterlife was similar to life on Earth. They filled tombs with things the dead might need in the afterlife. These included clothing, food, beds, games, and more. Ceremonial objects such as thrones, statues, and **jewelry** were also left in tombs.

King Tut became pharaoh around age nine. He died ten years later around 1323 BCE. The cause of his death is unknown. Some scientists think he died from a **chariot** crash. Others believe it was **malaria**.

King Tut's death mask was placed over his head and made to look like him. Ancient Egyptians believed it could guide King Tut's spirit back to his body.

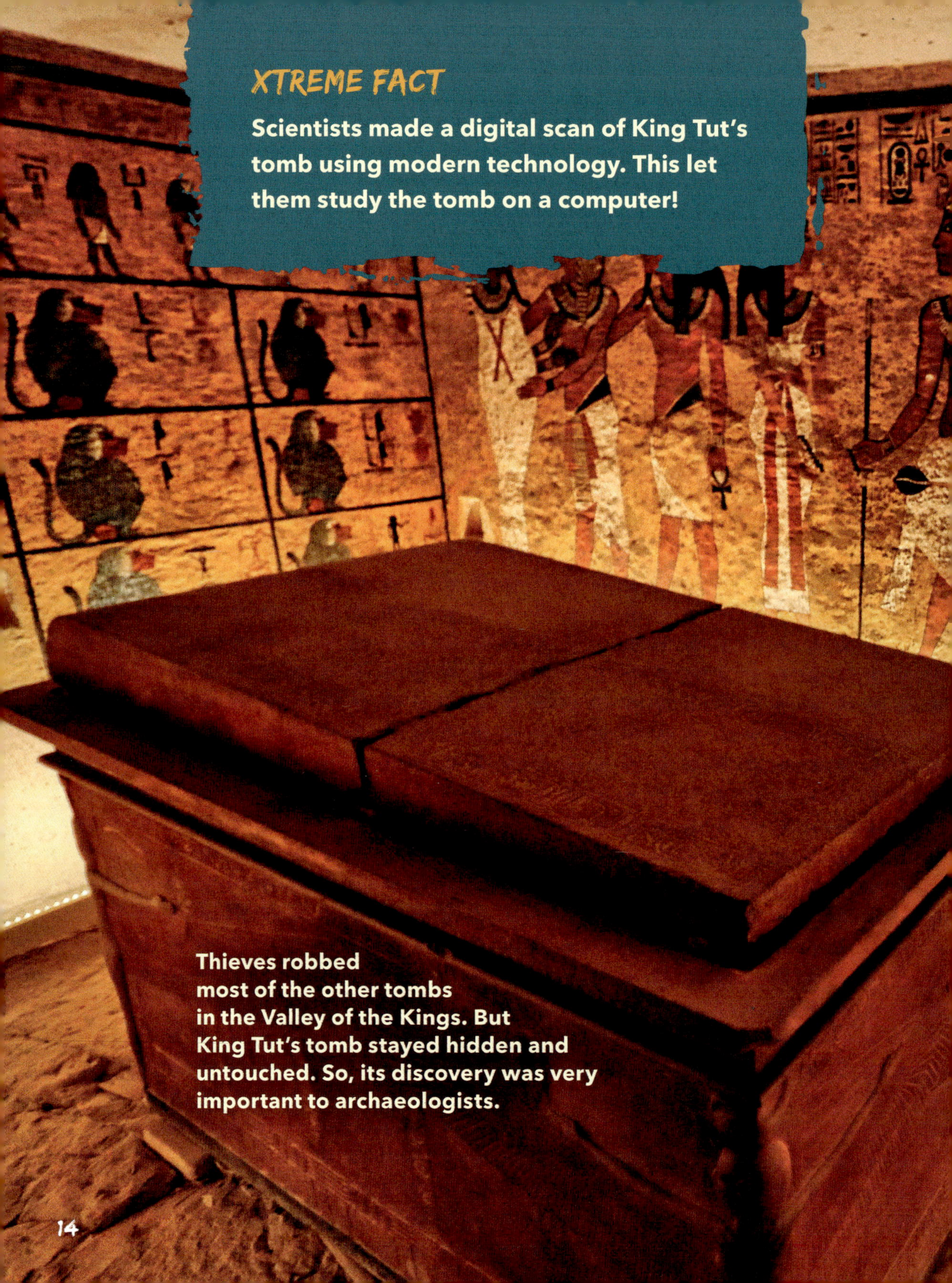

XTREME FACT

Scientists made a digital scan of King Tut's tomb using modern technology. This let them study the tomb on a computer!

Thieves robbed most of the other tombs in the Valley of the Kings. But King Tut's tomb stayed hidden and untouched. So, its discovery was very important to archaeologists.

Egyptologists and other scientists study King Tut's tomb. They continue exploring King Tut's life and death. This helps them learn about ancient Egypt's burial practices. They also work to preserve the tomb's **artifacts**.

CHAPTER 4

TOMB OF QIN SHI HUANG

The terra-cotta soldiers were buried in three pits. The first pit (*pictured*) is 203 feet (62 m) wide and 16 feet (5 m) deep.

Farmers were digging a well in Xi'an, China, in 1974. They found life-size soldiers made of terra-cotta, or baked clay. These statues led to the discovery of Qin Shi Huang's tomb compound. Qin Shi Huang was China's first emperor. He reigned until his death in 210 BCE.

XTREME FACT

Qin Shi Huang's actual tomb hasn't been opened. The people who built his tomb set up deadly traps to protect it. These include hidden crossbows, poisonous gas, and more!

Qin Shi Huang became emperor in 221 BCE. He wanted to live forever. So, he built an underground army for the afterlife. He believed the army would come to life and protect him after he died.

Qin Shi Huang (*center*) called himself Qin Shi Huangdi. This translates to "First August Emperor of Qin."

Each terra-cotta soldier stands 6 feet (1.8 m) tall and weighs about 400 pounds (181 kg). Many soldiers have their own features, clothing, and hairstyle.

Archaeologists found numerous terra-cotta statues in the tomb compound. These included more than 8,000 soldiers, 130 **chariots**, and 670 horses. They also found more than 40,000 bronze weapons. These included swords, lances, spears, and arrows. **Historians** believe more than 700,000 workers spent more than 30 years building the tomb compound.

Archaeologists use the tomb to learn about ancient Chinese society and burial practices. They study the tomb's soldiers. **Art historians** work to preserve the tomb compound. They also fix the terra-cotta statues.

Many artifacts from Qin Shi Huang's tomb are on display in the tomb compound's museum. The artifacts include a set of bronze horses with a chariot, a driver, and an umbrella.

CHAPTER 5

TOMB OF PAKAL THE GREAT

K'inich Janaab' Pakal, or Pakal the Great, was a **Maya** king. He ruled from 615 CE to 683 CE. When he died, he was buried under the Temple of the Inscriptions **pyramid** in modern Chiapas, Mexico.

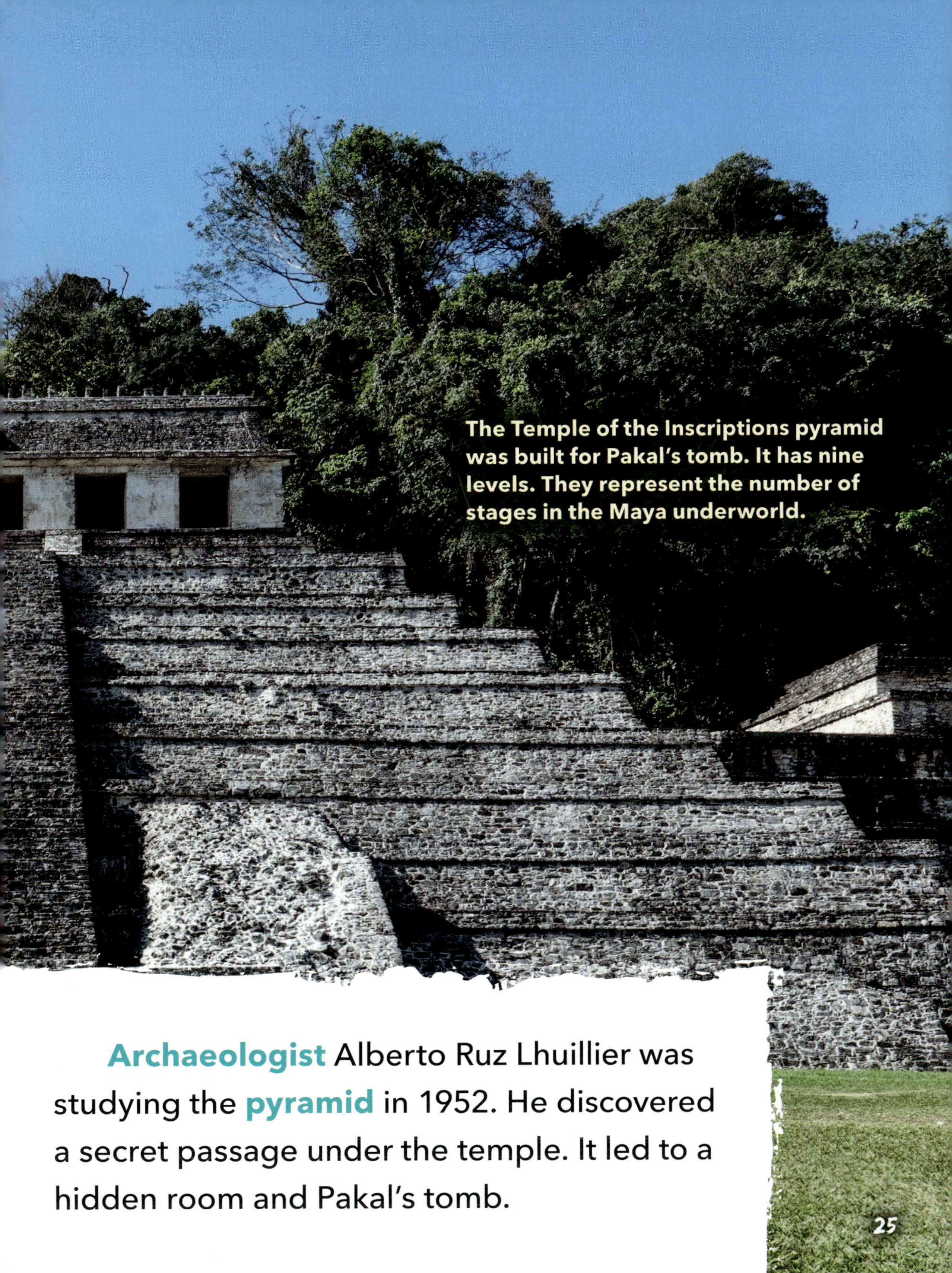

The Temple of the Inscriptions pyramid was built for Pakal's tomb. It has nine levels. They represent the number of stages in the Maya underworld.

Archaeologist Alberto Ruz Lhuillier was studying the **pyramid** in 1952. He discovered a secret passage under the temple. It led to a hidden room and Pakal's tomb.

Some people think the carvings on Pakal's **sarcophagus** lid show an astronaut or a time traveler. But the carvings are of Pakal and the World Tree. It showed his path to the gods and the **underworld**. The **Maya** believed the World Tree connected the underworld, the earthly world, and paradise.

Hieroglyphs, or ancient writing, found in Chiapas, Mexico. The Temple of the Inscriptions has 617 hieroglyphs on its inside walls. They recorded important events.

Pakal's sarcophagus lid weighed seven tons (6.4 t). Visitors can find a life-size copy (*pictured*) at the National Museum of Anthropology in Mexico City, Mexico.

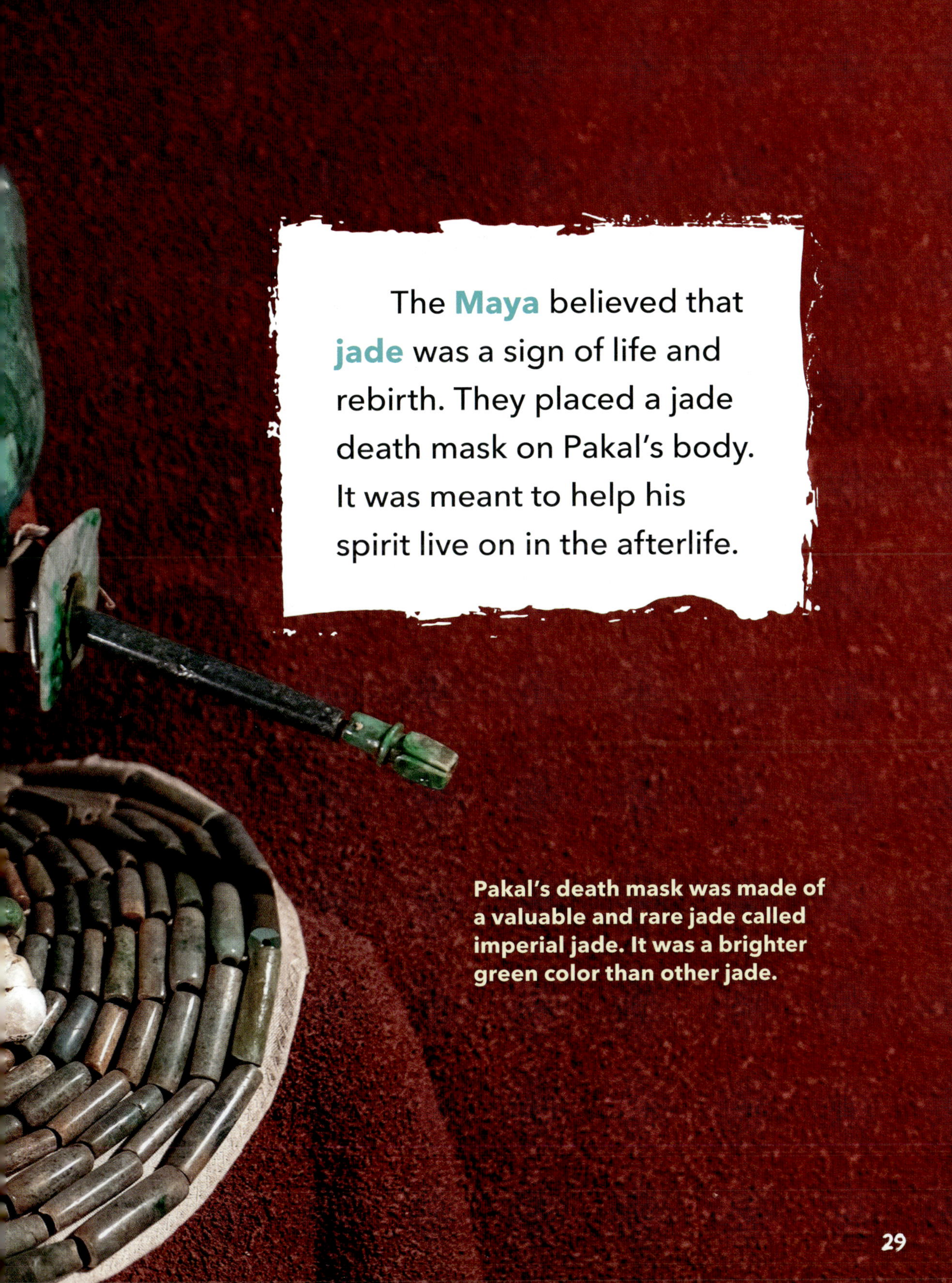

The **Maya** believed that **jade** was a sign of life and rebirth. They placed a jade death mask on Pakal's body. It was meant to help his spirit live on in the afterlife.

Pakal's death mask was made of a valuable and rare jade called imperial jade. It was a brighter green color than other jade.

Historians continue to explore Pakal's tomb and its carvings. **Archaeologists** study Pakal's remains. This helps them learn about Pakal's health and **Maya** society.

Historians learned that Pakal lived in the Palace of Palenque, which is next to the Temple of the Inscriptions. This is where he ruled from and held royal ceremonies.

CHAPTER 6

THE ROYAL TOMBS OF UR

In 1922, **archaeologist** Leonard Woolley found the Royal Tombs of Ur in modern Iraq. He uncovered around 1,800 graves over 12 years. The graves were created around 2600 BCE to 2500 BCE.

While digging, Woolley found 16 royal tombs. Each had a ramp leading underground. The tombs held **jewelry**, weapons, food, and seals carved with the person's name.

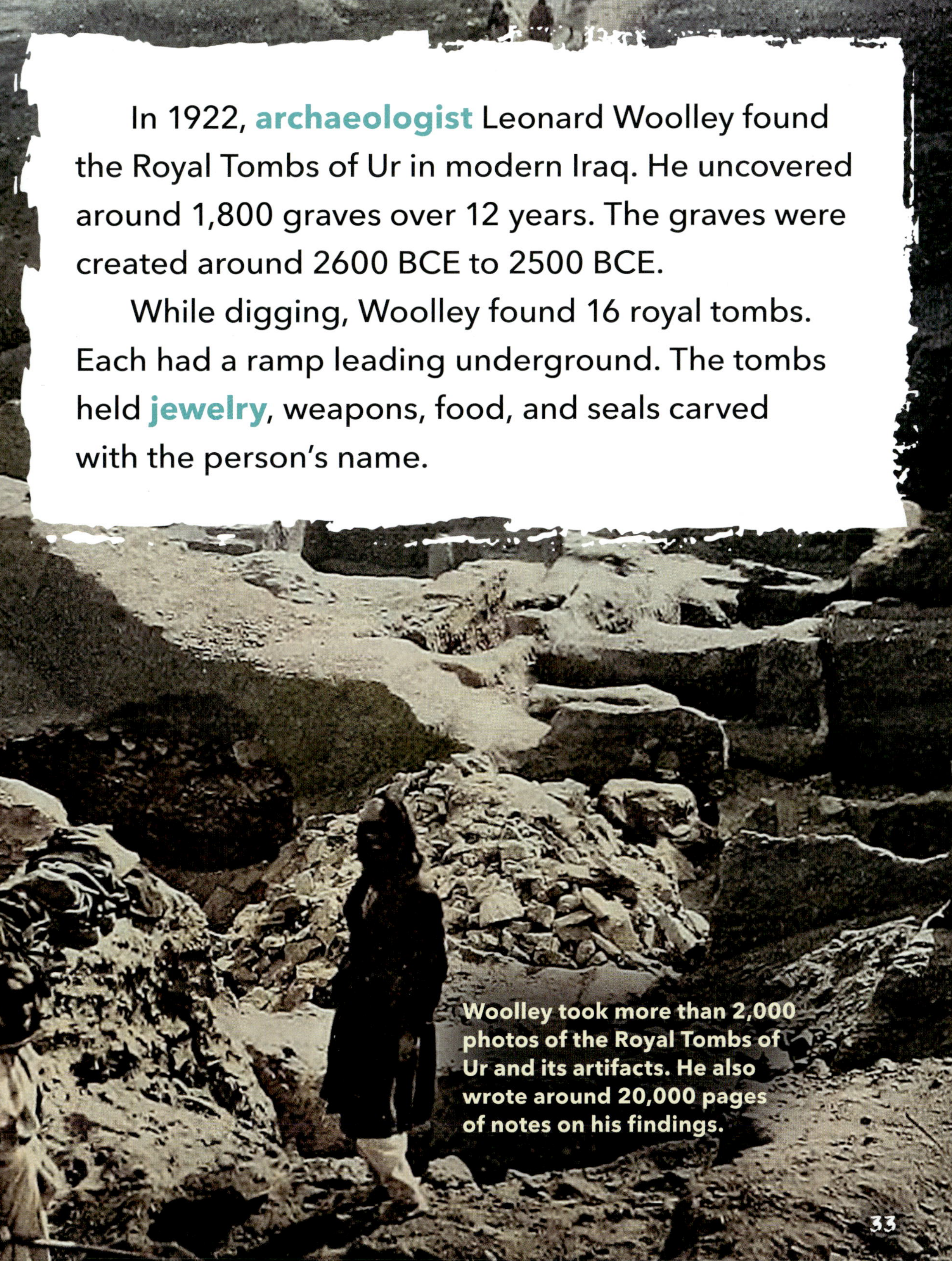

Woolley took more than 2,000 photos of the Royal Tombs of Ur and its artifacts. He also wrote around 20,000 pages of notes on his findings.

One of the Royal Tombs of Ur belonged to Queen Puabi. It held many artifacts, including a headdress (*right*) that was made of 20 gold leaves, gold ribbons, precious stone beads, and a large gold comb.

The ancient people of Ur built the tombs to honor the dead. They put objects into each tomb to help the dead in the afterlife. Many objects were made of gold, silver, and precious stones.

Queen Puabi's tomb also had a chariot, a small harp with a golden bull's head (*top*), a seal with her name (*bottom*), and more.

Efforts continue to preserve the Royal Tombs of Ur for history and education. Many scientists study the tombs. This helps them learn about the people of Ur and their burial practices, religion, royalty, early writing, and more.

The Royal Game of Ur was one of the artifacts found at the tombs. It's one of the oldest playable board games. The game's rules were found written on a tablet from 177 BCE.

THE TOMB OF THE UNKNOWN SOLDIER

The US military built the Tomb of the Unknown Soldier in Arlington, Virginia. They buried an unknown **World War I** soldier in it in 1921. In 1958, they added two crypts, or underground rooms where people are buried, in front of the Tomb. These were for the unknown soldiers from **World War II** and the **Korean War**. They later added a third crypt for an unknown soldier from the **Vietnam War**.

The final sarcophagus and surrounding structure were completed in 1932. The sarcophagus holds the World War I unknown soldier.

XTREME FACT

Scientists used modern technology to identify the Vietnam soldier's remains in 1998, and the soldier was reburied.

The east panel of the Tomb's sarcophagus shows three figures. They represent Peace (*left*), Victory (*center*), and Valor (*right*).

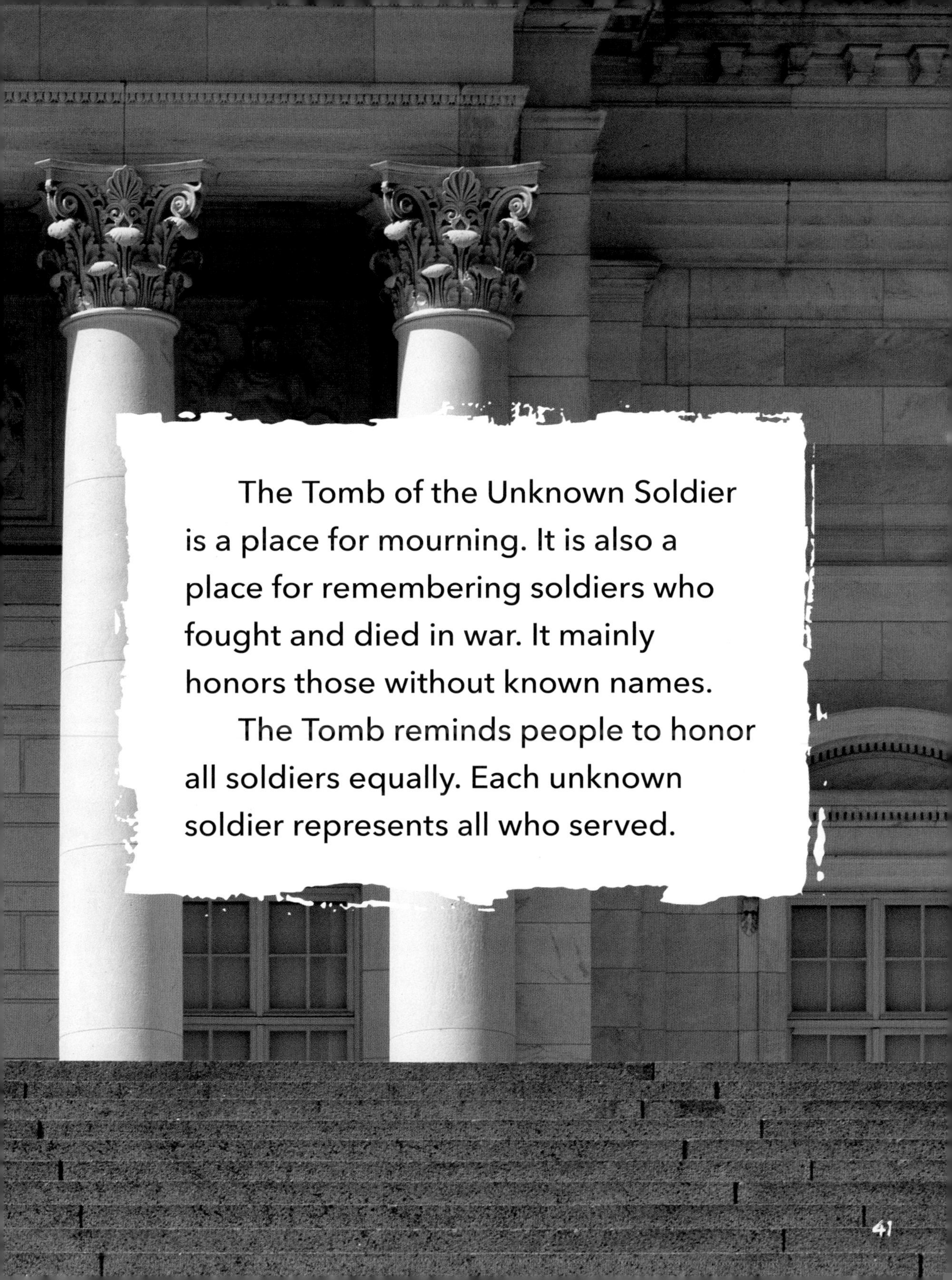

The Tomb of the Unknown Soldier is a place for mourning. It is also a place for remembering soldiers who fought and died in war. It mainly honors those without known names.

The Tomb reminds people to honor all soldiers equally. Each unknown soldier represents all who served.

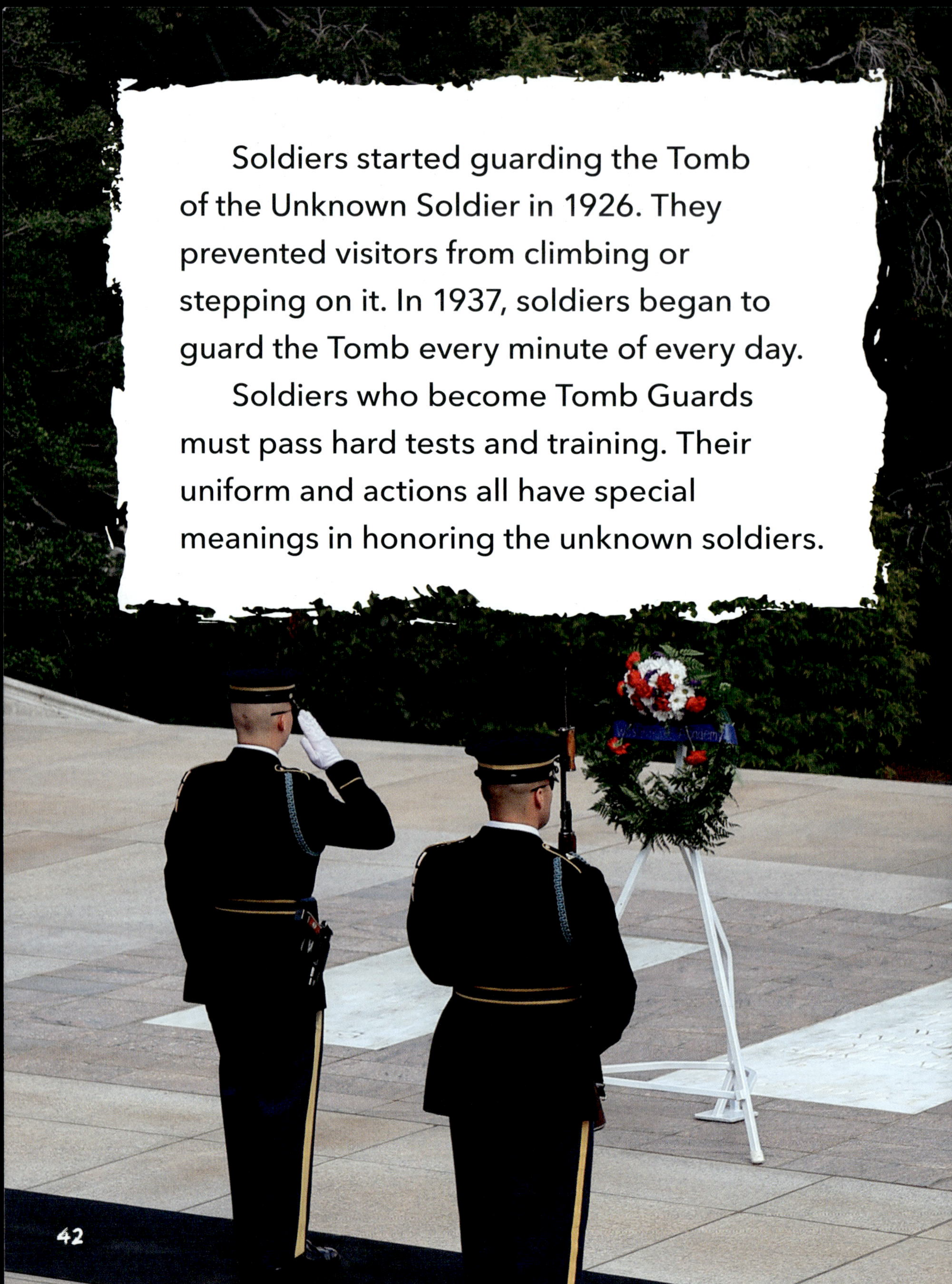

Soldiers started guarding the Tomb of the Unknown Soldier in 1926. They prevented visitors from climbing or stepping on it. In 1937, soldiers began to guard the Tomb every minute of every day.

Soldiers who become Tomb Guards must pass hard tests and training. Their uniform and actions all have special meanings in honoring the unknown soldiers.

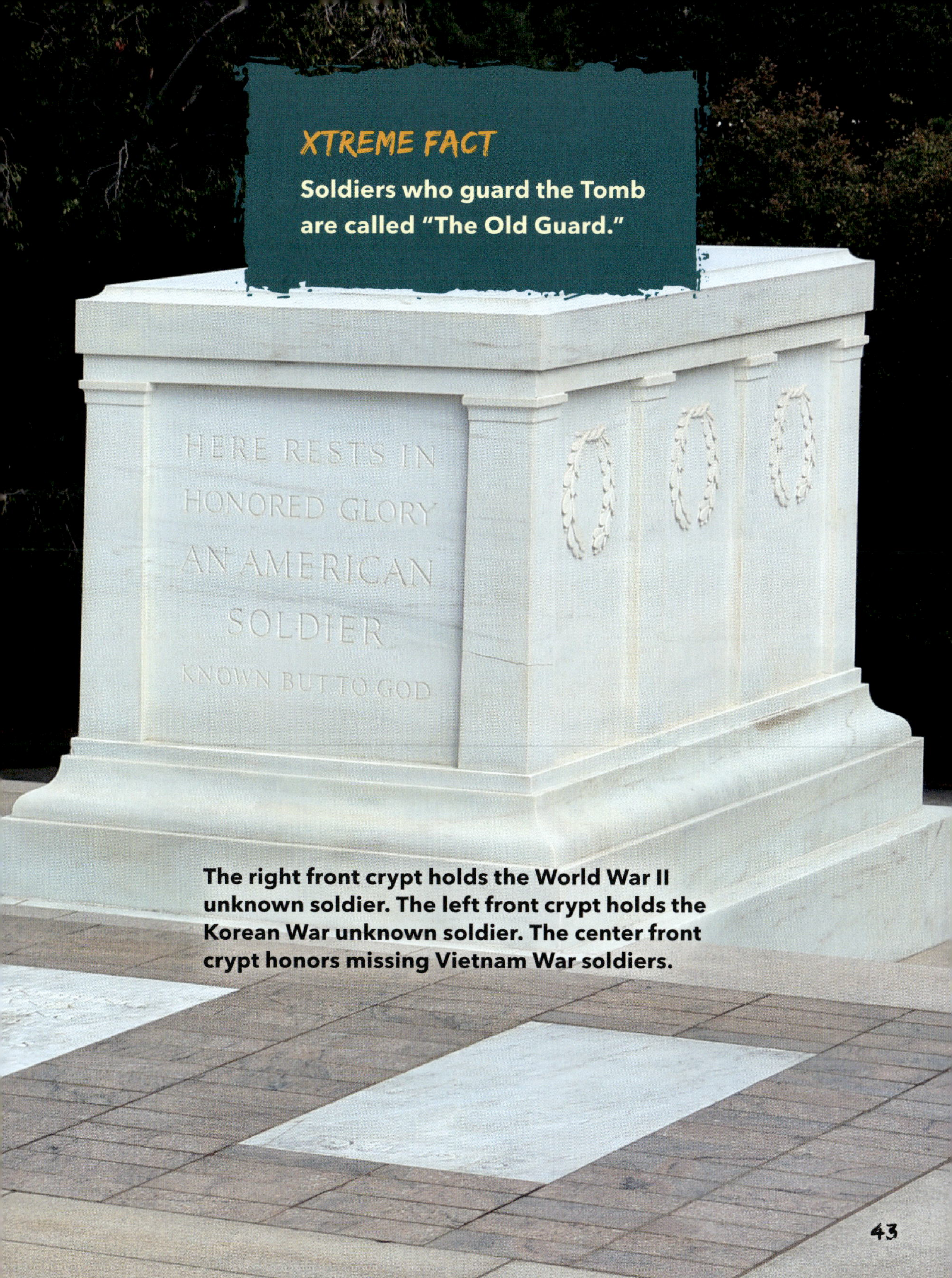

XTREME FACT

Soldiers who guard the Tomb are called "The Old Guard."

The right front crypt holds the World War II unknown soldier. The left front crypt holds the Korean War unknown soldier. The center front crypt honors missing Vietnam War soldiers.

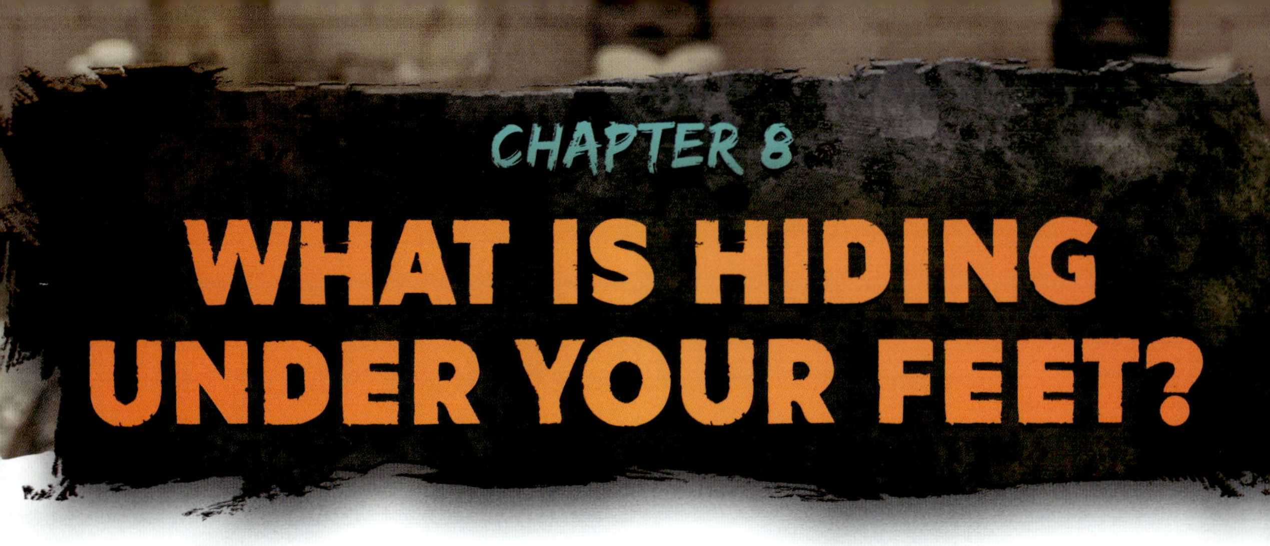

CHAPTER 8

WHAT IS HIDING UNDER YOUR FEET?

Scientists are still searching for undiscovered tombs and treasures worldwide. Every time one is found, it helps us learn about the people who lived a long time ago. The ground beneath our feet is full of mysteries just waiting to be explored!

Chinese historian Sima Qian wrote about Qin Shi Huang's burial chamber around 94 BCE. It's the only known record of what might be in the unopened burial chamber.

XTREME CHALLENGE

TAKE THE QUIZ BELOW AND PUT WHAT YOU'VE LEARNED TO THE TEST!

1) Why did people bury treasures in tombs?

2) What do tombs tell us about people that lived long ago?

3) Why do you think some tombs remain hidden for thousands of years?

4) What questions would you ask an ancient ruler about their tomb?

GLOSSARY

archaeologist–a person who studies the remains of ancient people and their activities.

art historian–a person who studies or writes about past artwork.

artifact–an object made by humans long ago for a practical purpose.

chariot–a small vehicle pulled by a horse, mostly used in ancient times.

Egyptologist–a person who studies the history, language, and culture of ancient Egypt, including its pharaohs, pyramids, and artifacts.

jade–a usually green mineral used as a gemstone.

jewelry–pretty things that are worn for decoration.

Korean War–from 1950 to 1953, fought in North and South Korea. The US government sent troops to help South Korea.

malaria–a deadly disease carried by mosquitoes.

Maya–an ancient Indigenous people who lived in Central America and Mexico from about 250 CE to 900 CE.

pyramid–a large ancient structure with a square base and four triangle walls that meet at the top.

sarcophagus–a stone or wooden coffin, often decorated, used to bury important people in ancient times.

underworld—in mythology, the place under the ground where the spirits of dead people go.

Vietnam War—from 1954 to 1975. A long, failed attempt by the United States to stop North Vietnam from taking over South Vietnam.

World War I—from 1914 to 1918, fought in Europe. Great Britain, France, Russia, the United States, and their allies were on one side. Germany, Austria-Hungary, and their allies were on the other side.

World War II—from 1939 to 1945, fought in Europe, Asia, and Africa. Great Britain, France, the United States, the Soviet Union, and their allies were on one side. Germany, Italy, Japan, and their allies were on the other side.

ONLINE RESOURCES

To learn more about tombs and treasures, please visit **abdobooklinks.com** or scan this QR code. These links are routinely monitored and updated to provide the most current information available.

INDEX